P9-DMV-140

FEEDING THE WORLD

Farmed Fish

Feeding the World

CORN

DAIRY PRODUCTS

EGGS

FARMED FISH

MEAT

RICE

SOY BEANS

WHEAT

FEEDING THE WORLD

Farmed Fish

KIM ETINGOFF

MASON CREST

Mason Crest
450 Parkway Drive, Suite D
Broomall, PA 19008
www.masoncrest.com

Printed and bound in the United States of America.

First printing
9 8 7 6 5 4 3 2 1

Series ISBN: 978-1-4222-2741-1
ISBN: 978-1-4222-2745-9
ebook ISBN: 978-1-4222-9077-4

The Library of Congress has cataloged the

hardcopy format(s) as follows:

Library of Congress Cataloging-in-Publication Data

Etingoff, Kim.
  Farmed fish / Kim Etingoff.
      p. cm. — (Feeding the world)
  ISBN 978-1-4222-2745-9 (hardcover) — ISBN 978-1-4222-2741-1 (series) — ISBN 978-1-4222-9077-4 (ebook)
  1. Fish culture—Juvenile literature. 2. Food supply—Juvenile literature. I. Title. II. Series: Feeding the world.
  SH151.E85 2014
  639.3—dc23
                                    2013004739

CONTENTS

FAMILY
PAK

PRICE:
$5.75

CHAPTER ONE

Where Does the Fish We Eat Come From?

Every food you eat has a story. At the end of the story, you eat the food. But the story of your food also has a beginning and middle.

If you know your food's story, you know where it comes from. You know who helped make that food. You know how it got to your plate.

THE BEGINNING

All food has one thing in common. It all comes from the earth. Food grows out of the ground and in the water.

But, you might think, a bag of chips doesn't come from the ground! That's only sort of true. Sure, there aren't any chip trees. You can't go out and pick a bag from a bush.

But all the ingredients in that bag of chips came from the earth. Chips are made out of potatoes. They also have salt in them. And vegetable oil.

The potatoes the chips are made out of grow under the ground. Farmers have to plant potatoes and help them grow on farms. Then they **harvest** the potatoes when they are big enough to eat.

Salt also comes from the ground. There are big salt mines around the world. People have to dig up salt under the earth. Then they clean it and grind it into small pieces. Some salt also comes from the ocean.

Vegetable oil comes from vegetables. Usually it's made from corn or soybeans. Corn and soybeans both grow on farms. The corn and soybeans get pressed hard until oil comes out.

All the other food you eat comes from the earth too. Every fruit and vegetable is a plant. So are grains like rice and oats. Grains are seeds from certain plants.

Even sugar is a plant. Sugar comes from plants called sugar cane or sugar beets. Other sugary things come from the earth too. Honey is made by bees. Maple syrup comes from inside maple trees.

Meat comes from animals. And animals are raised on farms. They eat grass, corn, and other plants (which all grow in the ground). Pork comes from pigs. Beef comes from cows. Chicken, of course, comes from chicken.

Dairy products (like cheese and ice cream) come from animals too. Cows and other animals give us milk. We can make foods like butter and yogurt out of that milk. Chickens give us eggs.

GROWING A GARDEN

If you really want to see where food comes from, try growing it yourself! Ask your paretns if you can start a garden in your yard. Or grow some vegetables in pots if you don't have room for a whole garden. When you grow a garden, you'll see what happens to fruits and vegetables from start to finish. First, you plant seeds. The seeds grow when they get water and sunlight. Then the plants keep getting bigger and bigger until they grow vegetables and fruits. Then you can harvest them and eat them. And you know just where they came from!

8   **Farmed Fish**

THE MIDDLE

After farmers grow the vegetables and raise the animals, food moves on to the next steps.

This is how the food gets to you. Different foods have to go through different steps to get to the grocery store.

Potato chips don't grow on trees or in the ground, but farmers are a big part of the story of chips. Farmers help make many of the ingredients in foods like chips, cookies, and more.

After the farm, a lot of food is sent to a factory. At the factory, it is **processed** into others foods. Processed means that it is cut up, cooked, and mixed with other things. This is where potatoes and salt and vegetable oil become chips.

What do you eat that's processed? Probably a lot of things. Milk gets mixed, added to, and heated up. Then it becomes cheese. Wheat (a grain) gets chopped into tiny pieces, smashed into flour, and mixed with sugar and eggs. Then it becomes a cookie.

Fresh fruits and vegetables look pretty much the same on the farm and in the store. They might only have to go through a couple of steps. They are washed. They are cut up. Maybe they're put into plastic packages.

After the factory, food has to get to the grocery store. Trucks, planes, boats, and trains take it from the factory. Then they bring the food to grocery store warehouses. Warehouses keep food until it goes to the store.

The fruits and vegetables farmers grow are sold at supermarkets or farmers' markets around the world. Sometimes, the food you buy comes from far away. Other times, you might buy food grown near where you live. Buying things at the supermarket or a farmers' market is the end of your food's story.

10 **Farmed Fish**

Farmers' Markets

Sometimes the grocery store is left out of a food's story. Farmers can sell what they grow to the people who eat the food. Often, they sell at something called a farmers' market. Lots of farmers come together and set up tables. They each sell whatever they grow or make—vegetables, fruits, meat, dairy, and more. People visit the farmers' market. They can talk to the farmers. They can see what their food looks like. Shopping at a farmers' market is a way to get your food right from the person who grew it.

THE END

This is where you come in. You and your family go to the store. You pick out what you want to buy. You take your food home and enjoy it.

At this point, it's hard to imagine where that food came from. Cans of green beans just look like cans. They don't look like green bean plants growing on a farm. But that's where they started out!

Your food could have come from all over the world. Maybe your mango came from Mexico. Your cereal might have been made out of grain from China. Your lettuce could have come from New Zealand.

The next time you go to the grocery store, think about the story of the food around you. Try to imagine where all those foods came from.

FIGURING OUT FISH

The fish we eat come from the earth too. Fish come from the oceans. They come from rivers and lakes and ponds. Fish also come from farms!

Fish don't grow on plants. They don't grow on farms with dirt and seeds. Farmers raising chickens, cows, or pigs don't usually raise fish. Fish grow on farms made out of water!

Fish farms could be giant tanks of water. They could be cages in the ocean or a lake. They could be ponds people made. There are many different kinds of fish farms.

Imagine all the fishing it would take to catch enough fish for hungry people around the world! To make things easier, people raise fish on farms. That way, farmers can raise many more fish than they could catch themselves.

12   Farmed Fish

Fish farms control how fish grow and make it easier to get them to hungry people. In the wild, people have to find fish to catch them. On one day, a fisher might catch 100 fish. The next day, she may not catch any.

On fish farms, farmers know just where the fish are. They don't have to look hard. They also can control how many fish they catch every day. Fish farms make it easier to send fish to grocery stores so people like you can eat them.

WILD FISH

Lots of the fish we eat are still caught in the wild. They live in the ocean or in a lake. People have to go out and catch them.

People have gotten really good at fishing in the wild. They have big boats and fancy nets. They know how to find fish pretty easily.

Today, more people want to eat fish than ever before. More and more people are being born every day. The earth holds a lot more people today than it used to. And lots of those people want to eat fish.

Fishers have been taking more and more fish out of the water. In fact, they've taken too many out. There aren't as many fish left in the ocean as there used to be.

If we keep fishing, there won't be many fish left. Lots of **species** will die out. That will mess things up in the oceans and rivers and lakes. And if we catch too many fish, then no one would get to eat them!

More people have turned to fish farming. On farms, people can control how many fish are born and how many are caught each day. If we raise more fish on farms, we don't have to take as many out of the wild.

Fish farming might be a way for us to keep eating fish in the future. But fish farming has also been going on for a long time.

CHAPTER TWO

The History of Farmed Fish

Fish farming has become really popular in the past few years. But it's nothing new. People have farmed fish for a long time.

THE FIRST FISH FARMS

Fish farms are thousands of years old. In China, people were farming fish 4,000 years ago. They farmed fish called carp.

The Chinese wrote down how they did it. Scientists and historians today can read the old writings. The writings prove that the **ancient** Chinese had fish farms. And they tell us how the ancient Chinese farmers raised fish.

Fish farmers in China caught baby carp in the wild. Then they moved them to special ponds. The carp grew up in the ponds. That's a little different from what happens today. It worked well for the Chinese fish farmers though.

Using fish eggs to start fish farms was a big change in the way people got the fish they eat. Many people around the world eat fish eggs by themselves too. The small, orange salmon eggs here are a big part of Japanese sushi.

16 **Farmed Fish**

In Ancient Rome, people farmed oysters like these. Inside their tough shell, oysters are a bit slimy. Many people love to eat these sea animals right out of the shell!

Other types of fish farms grew up in India, Egypt, and Rome. In the ancient Roman Empire, people farmed oysters, sea animals with thick shells. We still farm oysters today. Fish farming stretches back a long way!

CHANGES

It was a lot of work to catch all those baby fish, the way the ancient Chinese did. Farmers had to figure out ways to catch lots of fast-moving baby fish all at once. They also had to keep them alive as they took them out of the wild and put them in ponds. Fish die if they're out of the water too long.

People started looking for different ways to farm fish. They wanted it to be a little easier. A farmer in Germany came up with a new way to farm fish. He collected fish eggs instead of baby fish. The eggs were a lot easier to handle. They didn't swim away!

Modern fish farms, like this one in Bulgaria, raise fish so that we don't have to catch as many wild fish to eat. It's easier to farm fish than it is to find fish in the ocean!

He took as many eggs as he could find and put them all together. Then he **fertilized** them using male fish. Without fertilization, the eggs wouldn't hatch into baby fish.

The farmer raised the baby fish when they hatched. He put them in a pond. Then he fed them until they got big enough. Finally, he killed them and sold them to hungry people.

This is how many fish farmers still do it today. Over time, farmers have figured out how to raise fish in better ways. But they still start with eggs and end with fish.

MODERN FARMS

For a while, only a few people farmed fish. Most fish were caught in the wild. There were lots of fish in the sea. There wasn't really any need to raise them on farms.

The fish that you buy in the supermarket (like these salmon steaks) might come from a fish farm. You can find out where the fish your family buys came from by checking the package in the store or asking a waiter in a restaurant.

In the 1900s, people saw that farming fish was a good idea. There weren't as many fish in the oceans anymore. People had fished too much. Some people thought farms could raise as many fish as people wanted.

Today, about half of all the fish we eat are from farms. We will probably eat more and more fish from farms as fish in the wild disappear. Maybe farmers will even invent new and better ways to farm fish.

PEOPLE DISAGREE ABOUT FISH FARMS

Not everyone agrees that fish farms are a good idea. Some farms can hurt the environment. They are set up in places that hurt natural areas. Sometimes fish farms **pollute** water.

Some people worry that fish farms hurt other fish living nearby. They say that the farmed fish make the water unhealthy for wild fish. They also say that farming fish doesn't really solve the problem of people taking too many fish out of the wild, because some fish need to eat other fish.

20 Farmed Fish

Another problem is that fish farming doesn't always replace catching fish in the wild. They actually might make more fish disappear in the wild.

Once in a while, fish escape farms. They get into lakes and rivers and oceans. Those escaped fish might be sick. When they meet wild fish, they can spread their sickness. Lots of wild fish could die.

Some farm fish, like salmon, eat other fish. Farmers have to feed them fish. But they don't raise the fish that salmon eat on farms. They catch them in the wild. Farmed salmon eat wild fish. That just adds to the problem of fish disappearing from the oceans as people catch more and more.

Other fish are better to raise on farms. Some fish, like tilapia, don't eat other fish. They can eat food that comes from vegetables. That means that we don't have to take fish out of the ocean to feed the farm fish.

Other people hope that fish farming can solve our fish problem. They think we can figure out how to set up fish farms that are healthy and don't hurt the environment. That way, we can let more wild fish live.

FISH TO EAT, FISH TO AVOID

Here's a list of just some of the fish that have been disappearing from the wild: cod, groupers, monkfish, salmon, sturgeon, swordfish, and tuna. When you're getting fish, think about which fish you're eating.

CHAPTER THREE

Who Raises the Farmed Fish We Eat?

When you think of a farmer, what do you think of? You probably think of someone growing vegetables or raising animals on land. You might think of a farmer working hard to make sure his vegetables grow big. You might think of a farmer milking his cows.

We can also think of people who raise fish. Sure, they don't drive tractors or plant seeds. But they do **produce** food.

Any person who raises living things for food is a farmer. Farmers raise many different kinds of things. Farmers could raise fruit. Or grains. Or cows. Farmers can also raise fish!

HOW MANY FARMERS?

Fish farming is popular. Not too long ago, there weren't many fish farmers. But today, over 16 million people are fish farmers. That's a lot of people!

Every year, there are more and more fish farmers. People see that it's a good way to grow and sell food.

Fish farmers work all around the world. Fish are farmed in Asia, Europe, and North America. Fish farmers may work in the ocean, like the farmers here, or work on fish farms on land.

24 **Farmed Fish**

Fish farmers have a big job. They have to make sure that the fish they raise are healthy and good to eat. Fish farmers have to know a lot about fish to do their jobs well!

In fact, fish farming is growing faster than all other farm jobs. There are more new fish farmers every year than any other kind of farmer. Pretty soon, there will be lots more fish farmers than there are today.

FISH FARM JOBS

The farmer has a lot to do on a fish farm. He has to take care of fish eggs. He has to make sure baby fish are fed and grow fast. He has to take care of sick fish. And he has to kill the fish so we can eat them.

There are also jobs that don't have much to do with handling fish or making sure they make good food. Farming is more than just growing things. Farmers have to keep track of how much money they're spending. They have to figure out what they can buy for the farm with the money they have.

If a farmer needs a new **tank** for fish eggs, she can't spend too much on it. But she also has to get a good tank too, one that won't break. She'll have to choose which tank to buy. It can be a tough choice!

Who Raises the Farmed Fish We Eat?   25

Farmers with few fish might have to take their fish to the market themselves. On farms with more fish, the fish might end up at a big fish market or supermarket.

Farmers also have to figure out where to sell their fish. They can't just raise them and let them go to waste.

Farmers have to work with suppliers—people who sell fish to stores. They also talk to grocery stores and truck companies. Farmers have to figure out where their fish will go when they leave the farm.

If the fish farm is really small, the farmer probably does a lot of the work. There might be just one person running the whole farm. He has to take care of the fish. He has to take it to a market. He makes all of the money from selling the fish.

26   Farmed Fish

Fish farms are different all around the world. These fish farmers from China have a different way of doing things from fish farmers in other parts of the world. More fish farmers work in China than in any other country in the world.

On bigger farms, one person can't do everything. There's just too much to do! One farmer might be in charge of taking care of the eggs. Another farmer probably watches over the baby fish. A farmer has to feed the big fish before they're killed and sold.

Other people take care of the farm's money. They figure out where to sell the fish and how it will get there. They work to get the best prices on things the farm needs to buy. They also work to get the most amount of money for the fish the farm sells.

Who Raises the Farmed Fish We Eat? 27

This fish farm is in Vietnam. Most fish is sold in the country where it's farmed because fish doesn't stay fresh for long. Some fish travels around the world to be sold, though.

28 **Farmed Fish**

FISH FARMING AROUND THE WORLD

Fish farms are popular all over the world. But some countries have more fish farms than others.

China produces the most farmed fish in the world. About 70 percent of the world's farmed fish come from China. That means that 7 out of 10 farm fish are raised in China. That's a lot!

China was one of the first places where people farmed fish. And it's still going strong.

India raises the next biggest number of fish. A lot of the other countries that produce farm fish are also in Asia, near China and India.

People in Asia eat more fish than people in other parts of the world. It makes sense that there's more fish farming there. If people want fish, then farmers will set up fish farms.

Lots of people in Africa are choosing to farm fish too. Africans eat a lot of fish. So raising fish can make farmers money. The number of fish farmers in Africa is growing every day. Fish farming is growing faster in Africa than in any other part of the world.

From South Africa to Zambia to Nigeria, farmers are setting up fish farms. Soon, these fish farmers may be feeding people around the world.

CHAPTER FOUR

How Are Farmed Fish Raised?

Vegetable farms have rows and rows of plants growing in the ground. There might be tractors and bags of seeds. Farms raising cows have fences and big barns where the cows can be milked. But what does a fish farm look like?

Fish farms come in all different types. Some are in the ocean. Some are small tanks as far from the ocean as you can get. There are also many other kinds of fish farms.

TYPES OF FARMS

Some fish farms are just simple ponds. They could be **manmade** ponds. Or they could be natural ponds. The ponds can be fresh water or saltwater. Rivers and lakes are fresh water. That means the water has no salt in it. Oceans are saltwater. Some fish can only live in fresh water. Some can only live in saltwater.

Fish are kept in the ponds for their whole lives. Tilapia, catfish, and shrimp are often raised in ponds.

Some fish farms have many tanks for fish. These tanks have to be kept clean so that the fish inside grow up healthy. A lot of work goes into keeping the water in the tanks clean.

32   **Farmed Fish**

These workers are building a tank for a fish farm. There are many kinds of fish farms around the world, some on land and some in the ocean. Some fish are raised in nets, others in tanks like the ones being built here.

Sometimes the easiest way to farm fish is to keep them in cages or nets. The cages are in the ocean or in a lake. The fish don't really live in the wild, but they get to swim in the kind of water they are used to. The fish can't swim freely or get out. They stay inside the cages.

There are a few problems with keeping the fish in these cages or nets. Once in a while, fish can escape from nets and cages. If that happens, the farmer loses the fish and can't sell them. Fish waste (poop) can also get into the water around the cages. That can pollute the ocean or lake if there are too many fish in one area.

Fish can also live in indoor tanks. The tanks have to be big to raise a lot of fish! Salmon, sturgeon, and bass can live in tanks.

In tanks, the water gets taken out and cleaned and put back in all the time. The fish live in clean water. They don't pollute the ocean. Tanks cost a lot to run, though. Not all farmers can afford them. Many farmers just don't have the money to buy tanks that cost a lot.

Farmers also raise shellfish. Shellfish are clams, oysters, and mussels. They don't move around much. Farmers raise them differently.

Farmers can hang ropes in the ocean. The ropes have shellfish on them. Shellfish just stick in one place, so they're easy to raise. Farmers don't have to worry about them escaping. They can grow the shellfish in the ocean.

FISH RANCHING

Ranches usually have cows on them. You might think of cowboys when you think of ranches. You probably don't think of fish farmers!

But some fish farmers are actually fish ranchers. First, the farmers hatch the fish from eggs. When the fish are small, the farmers have to train them to come when called. They play a sound whenever they feed the fish. The fish learn that when they hear that sound, they get fed.

After a while, farmers let the fish go into the wild. Whenever the farmer plays the sound, the fish will come back. They want something to eat!

FISH HEARING

Fish ears are kind of like the ears people have, just not on the outside of their heads. Fish can hear pretty well in water. Sound travels faster through water than air. And water can be hard to see through. Fish use sound to find food and stay away from bigger animals that want to eat them. In fish ranching, farmers use sound to call the fish back to the ranch.

Farmers don't have to feed their fish most of the time. In fish ranching, the fish can swim freely. They catch food for themselves in the wild.

When the fish get big enough to eat, the farmer calls them back one more time. This time, they are caught and killed. After that, they're sent to the grocery store or market for people to buy and eat.

Some farms buy young fish from fish hatcheries. Fish hatcheries like this one raise the fish early on and then sell the fish to farms. Then the farms raise the fish until they are ready to go to the market.

How Are Farmed Fish Raised? 35

Fish farming takes a lot of water. These pumps keep clean water coming into the farm to replace water that's old or dirty.

BABIES

In order to get big fish, you first have to have babies. Farmers are in charge of hatching eggs into baby fish.

First, big fish lay eggs. Depending on how many fish are on the farm, there could be millions of eggs. The farmers take the eggs and put them in a special place to hatch.

When the eggs hatch, the babies are called fry. They don't look much like their parents yet. The fry are put into tanks or in a place away from the big fish. That's because their parents might eat them!

The farmer feeds the fry. They need to eat a lot of food so that they grow bigger. As they get bigger, they are called fingerlings.

FOOD

The biggest thing farmers have to do is feed their fish. What a fish eats depends on what kind of fish it is.

Some fish eat tiny creatures in the ocean. Farmers can just keep the fish in cages in the ocean. They catch the tiny creatures that happen to be swimming by. They can feed themselves. Tilapia, for example, eat tiny things called phytoplankton.

Shellfish eat tiny water creatures. In fact, farmers don't even have to feed shellfish. They just raise shellfish in the ocean. The shellfish can feed themselves by filtering the water that passes by.

Other fish eat bigger animals—mostly other fish. Farmers can feed them actual fish. Or they can give them pellets made out of ground-up fish. Most fish eat other fish. They are carnivores. Carnivores are animals that eat meat.

CLEAN WATER

Lots of fish in one place produce a lot of poop. Farmers want to keep the water clean. That way, the fish won't get sick.

Closed-in farms need a way to clean the water. Tanks and ponds are closed-in farms. Farmers can get cleaning systems. They can cost a lot of money. But they're important. No farmer wants his fish to get sick. Sick fish don't make good food!

If the fish farm is a cage in the ocean, or a net in a river, farmers don't have to clean the water. The fish waste drifts off into the ocean or river or lake.

This isn't good for the environment. Too much fish waste pollutes the water. It makes other living things nearby sick.

Shellfish can help clean the water. Putting them with other fish can be a good idea. They **filter** the water.

Keeping the water clean on fish farms is a big part of raising fish. Keeping the water clean helps to keep fish healthy.

CHAPTER FIVE

How Do Fish Get to Your Plate?

Now you know how fish are raised on farms. But the story of the fish you eat isn't over yet. The fish still need to get from the farm to you.

PROCESSING

Once the fish get big enough, it's time to send them on the way to **customers** around the world.

First, fish have to be killed before we eat them. All meat comes from living animals. If we're going to eat them, we have to kill them. Often, farmers kill fish by putting them in cold water.

Next, the fish have to be cut up. Sometimes fish are sent whole to grocery stores. But often, they're cut into pieces.

The farmer or farmworkers take out the fish's insides. They cut the head and tail off.

Some of the fish are cut into fillets. Fillets are what people often see in the grocery store. They are pieces of fish. They don't look like whole fish.

Fish has to be farmed, cleaned, cut up, and moved to the place it's going to be sold. By the end of the story, you might not even know the meat you're buying is fish!

40 Farmed Fish

Whenever you see a sign for "Fresh Fish," remember that doesn't mean that the fish were raised at the store! The fish you eat has a long story before it gets to the supermarket.

Many fish farms use machines to process the fish. On smaller farms, farmworkers might do it all themselves with knives.

ON THE MOVE

The farmers have to get their fish from the farm to the store or market. Fish might travel many miles to get to the people who are buying them. Usually, farmers move their fish on a truck.

The truck will take the fish to the next step. Sometimes fish have even farther to go. The truck takes the fish to an airport or a harbor. Then the fish are loaded onto a plane or boat. The plane or boat takes the fish to a different part of the world. Your fish could come from halfway around the planet!

Soon, the fish makes its way to a warehouse or a market. Warehouses keep food, like fish, until it's ready to go to the store. Once at the warehouse or market, the truck unloads all its fish.

Fish has to be kept cold while it's moved from place to place. The large trucks used to move fish to the supermarket have large refrigerators on them. That way, the fish will be good even if it has to travel a long way from the farm to the store.

42 **Farmed Fish**

Fish are sold in supermarkets and fish markets. People around the world can enjoy eating fish thanks to fish farmers. Many people are part of the story of the fish you buy at the market, from farmers to truck drivers to the people who work at the store.

The workers at the warehouse sort the fish into different places. Not all of the fish will end up in the same place.

Some of the fish is sent to one grocery store an hour away. Some of it is sent to a grocery store an hour away in a different direction. And some of it is sent to your grocery store.

After all that, customers like you go to the store. They go to the fish section and pick out their fish. Most people never think twice about how far that fish had to come to get there. It was a long trip!

All of this has to happen very fast. Fish don't last long. They go bad and then we can't eat them. At most, there are a few days between when the fish leave the farm and when people are eating them.

KEEPING THE FISH COLD

Fish have to be kept cold at all times. If a dead fish gets too warm, **bacteria** could start growing on it. Then it would make you sick if you ate it.

Once fish are killed, they have to be cold all the time. They have to be kept cold when they're being cut up. They have to be cold when they're put into trucks. Fish need to be kept cold when they are moved to the grocery store. They have to be cold in the store. And they have to be cold once they make it into your home.

The next time you eat fish at home or walk by the fish section in the store, use your imagination. Picture where that fish came from and who helped get it there.

Now that you know more about your food, you can make better food choices. Do you think eating farmed fish is a good idea? Should we eat wild fish too? It's up to you and your family how you want to eat!

<u>LABELS</u>

Some fish have labels on them that say where they came from. They'll say if the fish was raised on a farm or was caught in the wild. It might even say what country it came from. Take a look at the package the next time you buy fish. Or ask a worker at the grocery store. If you're ordering fish in a restaurant, ask the waiter or waitress.

WORDS TO KNOW:

ancient: Very old or from a much earlier time in history.

bacteria: Tiny creatures so small you can't see them. Some can make people sick, but most don't, and some even help keep people healthy.

customers: People who buy things, including food.

dairy products: Foods made from milk (like cheese, butter, ice cream, and more).

fertilized: When fish eggs have what they need to hatch into baby fish.

filter: To clean or take out dirty parts.

harvest: Gathering grown plants on a farm.

manmade: Made or built by people.

pollute: To make dirty or hurt the environment.

processed: The way ingredients are mixed or changed in a factory to produce the foods we eat.

produce: To make or gather to sell to others.

species: Kinds of animals.

tank: A container that can be filled with water or other things.

FIND OUT MORE

ONLINE

Fish and Farming Regulation and Control
vafd.gov.mt/info-for-kids

Seafood Watch
www.montereybayaquarium.org/cr/seafoodwatch.aspx

Where does this food come from?
www.1millionacts.com.au/inspiration/kids-quiz-where-does-this-food-come-from

IN BOOKS

Gibbons, Gail. *The Vegetables We Eat*. New York: Holiday House, 2007.

Pollan, Michael. *The Ominvore's Dilemma (Young Reader's Edition)*. New York: Penguin, 2009.

Reilly, Kathleen M. *Food: 25 Amazing Projects*. White River Junction, Ver.: Nomad Press, 2010.

INDEX

ABOUT THE AUTHOR

Kim Etingoff lives in Boston, Massachusetts, spending part of her time working on farms. Kim enjoys connecting people of all ages to agriculture and teaching others where their food comes from.

PICTURE CREDITS